Nonfiction Readers®

The Story of the White House

By Marge Kennedy

Children's Press®
An Imprint of Scholastic Inc.
New York Toronto London Auckland Sydney
Mexico City New Delhi Hong Kong
Danbury, Connecticut

These content vocabulary word builders are for grades 1–2.

Subject Consultant: Eli J. Lesser, MA, Director of Education, National Constitution Center, Philadelphia, Pennsylvania

Reading Consultant: Cecilia Minden-Cupp, PhD, Early Literacy Consultant and Author, Chapel Hill, North Carolina

Photographs © 2009: Alamy Images: 5 bottom right, 7 main (Yvonne Duffe), 4 bottom left, 12 (Art Kowalsky), 5 top left, 10 (North Wind Picture Archives), 20, 21 (PCL); Corbis Images: 2, 5 bottom left, 14, 15 top, 15 bottom (Brooks Kraft), 23 top right; Danita Delimont Stock Photography/Lisa S. Engelbrecht: 23 bottom right; Getty Images: 5 top right, 13, 18 (Altrendo Travel), 6 (Peter Gridley); Courtesy of the Harry S. Truman Library and Museum: back cover, 4 top, 16, 17 bottom, 17 top; Library of Congress/George Munger & William Strickland: 1, 11, 23 top left; Pennsylvania Academy of the Fine Arts: 7 inset; Photo Researchers, NY/Erich Schrempp: 4 bottom right, 8; PictureHistory.com: 23 bottom left; Superstock, Inc.: 19 (age fotostock), cover (Ping Amranand); The Granger Collection, New York/Benjamin H. Latrobe: 9.

Scholastic Inc., 557 Broadway, New York, NY 10012.

Series Design: Simonsays Design!
Art Direction, Production, and Digital Imaging: Scholastic Classroom Magazines

Library of Congress Cataloging-in-Publication Data

Kennedy, Marge M., 1950-
The Story of the White House / Marge Kennedy.
    p. cm. – (Scholastic news nonfiction readers)
Includes bibliographical references and index.
ISBN 13: 978-0-531-21094-9 (lib. bdg.)   978-0-531-22431-1 (pbk.)
ISBN 10: 0-531-21094-4 (lib. bdg.)   0-531-22431-7 (pbk.)
1. White House (Washington, D.C.)–Juvenile literature. 2. White House (Washington, D.C.)–History–Juvenile literature. 3. Presidents–United States–History–Juvenile literature. 4. Washington (D.C.)–Buildings, structures, etc.–Juvenile literature. I. Title.
F204.W5K456 2009
975.3–dc22   2008037424

CONTENTS

WORD HUNT

Look for these words as you read. They will be in **bold**.

carpenters
(**kar**-pen-turz)

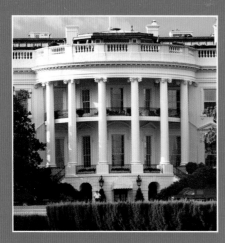

porch
(porch)

sandstone
(**sand**-stohn)

4

fire
(fire)

flagpole
(**flag**-pohl)

West Wing
(west wing)

White House
(wite houss)

A House That Changes

The **White House** is where the President lives and works. It is more than 200 years old. But the White House has not always looked like it does today.

White House

George Washington, our first President, died before the White House was finished.

At first, the White House was not white! The builders used **sandstone**, a gray and brown stone, to build it.

Then the house was painted white. People started calling it the White House.

sandstone

This is an early drawing of the White House.

of the Presidents House, with the addition of the North and South Porti

The White House was burned in a **fire** when it was still new. After the fire, only the walls were left. It took three years to build the White House again.

fire

This is how the White House looked after the fire, in 1814.

Over time, our country grew. So did the White House!

New Presidents added new rooms. One added a **porch** to one side. Another added a porch to the other side.

porch

This porch is called the North Portico.

Theodore Roosevelt added a whole building. It is called the **West Wing**. He had six noisy children. He wanted a new, quiet place to work. The President's office is in the West Wing today.

West Wing

The West Wing is connected to the main house by a walkway.

The White House started to fall apart as it got older. In 1948, the President and his family had to move out.

Carpenters and other workers came to fix the White House. It took them four years.

carpenters

President Truman's family lived nearby while the White House was rebuilt.

Today the new White House stands strong. The American flag flies on the **flagpole** whenever the President is at home.

With every new President, the story of the White House goes on.

flagpole

The White House is painted every few years to keep it white.

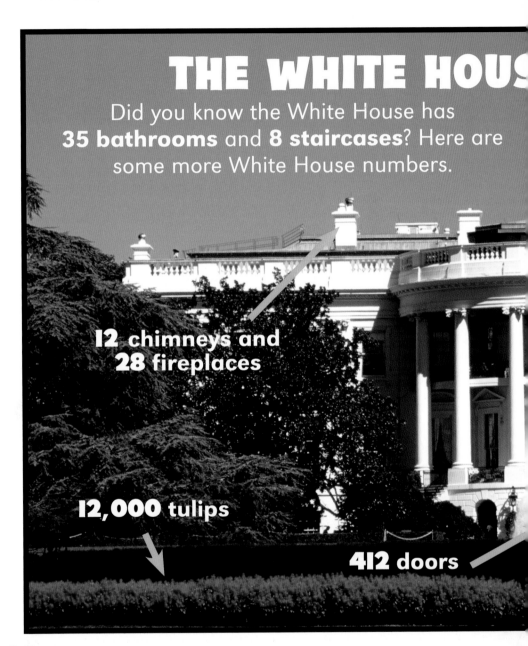

THE WHITE HOUS

Did you know the White House has **35 bathrooms** and **8 staircases**? Here are some more White House numbers.

12 chimneys and **28** fireplaces

12,000 tulips

412 doors

Y THE NUMBERS

570 gallons of white paint cover the outside.

147 windows

132 rooms

YOUR NEW WORDS

carpenters (**kar**-pen-turz) people who build and fix things made of wood

fire (fire) flames, light, and heat that come from burning something

flagpole (**flag**-pohl) a tall pole for raising and flying a flag

porch (porch) an area with a roof attached to the outside of a building

sandstone (**sand**-stohn) a gray and brown rock with a grainy surface

West Wing (west wing) a building connected to the White House. The President and his staff work there.

White House (wite houss) the home and workplace of the U.S. President

THE WHITE HOUSE FROM 1814 TO TODAY

1814

About 1860

About 1905

Today

INDEX

FIND OUT MORE
Book:
Waters, Kate. *The Story of the White House*. New York: Scholastic Paperbacks, 1992.

Website:
Enchanted Learning
www.enchantedlearning.com/history/us/monuments/whitehouse

MEET THE AUTHOR
Marge Kennedy has written five other books about the White House.